Welcome to the Home Study Collection,™ create(
the home is a child's first and most im

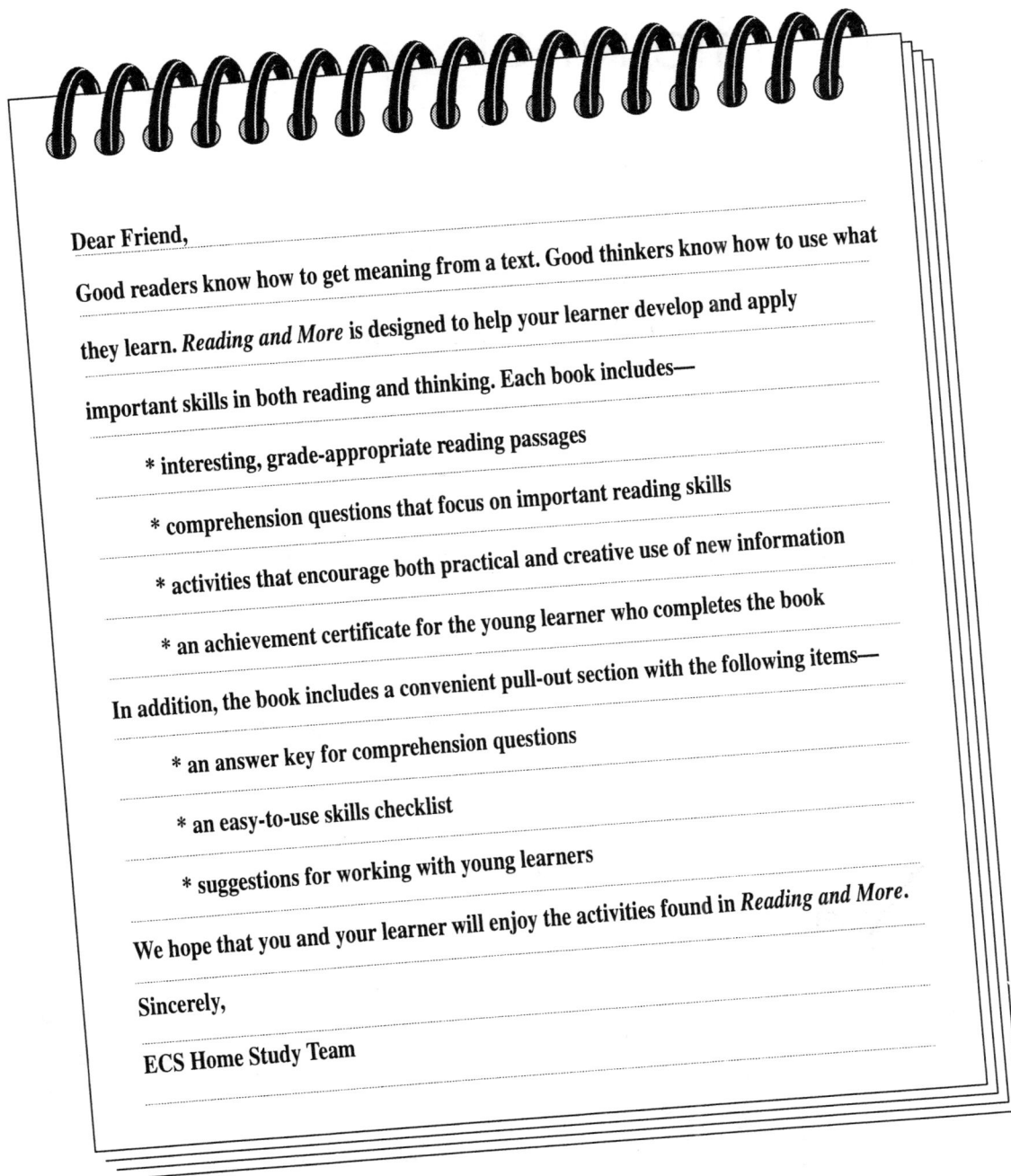

MW01528089

Dear Friend,

Good readers know how to get meaning from a text. Good thinkers know how to use what they learn. *Reading and More* is designed to help your learner develop and apply important skills in both reading and thinking. Each book includes—

* interesting, grade-appropriate reading passages

* comprehension questions that focus on important reading skills

* activities that encourage both practical and creative use of new information

* an achievement certificate for the young learner who completes the book

In addition, the book includes a convenient pull-out section with the following items—

* an answer key for comprehension questions

* an easy-to-use skills checklist

* suggestions for working with young learners

We hope that you and your learner will enjoy the activities found in *Reading and More.*

Sincerely,

ECS Home Study Team

ISBN 1-57022-021-2
Edited by Lori Mammen
Page Layout and Graphics by Lisa Avitia and Julie Gumm
Cover and Book design by Educational Media Services
Art on pages 17, 20, 26, 33, 36, 40, 42, 50, 51, 52 by Corel GALLERY

# Three Little Kittens

Three little kittens lost their mittens
And they began to cry,
"Oh, mother dear, we sadly fear
Our mittens we have lost."
"What? Lost your mittens, you **naughty** kittens!
Then you shall have no pie."
"Meow, meow, meow, meow,"
"No, you shall have no pie."

The three little kittens found their mittens,
And they began to cry,
"Oh, mother dear, see here, see here,
Our mittens we have found."
"Put on your mittens, you good little kittens,
And you shall have some pie."
"Purr, purr, purr, purr,
Oh, let us have some pie."

**Directions:** Circle or write the answer to the following questions about the nursery rhyme.

1.  The three little kittens got in trouble because they—

    were fighting

    lost their mittens

    ate the pie

2.  The word **naughty** means—

    good     happy     bad

3.  The three little kittens could not have pie because—

    they lost their mittens

    they found their mittens

    they were crying

4.  The mother cat gave the kittens pie after they found their mittens.

    Yes     No

5.  What sound did the kittens make when they were happy?

    _____

- Pretend that you are one of the kittens. Act out part of the story for your family. First, act like you lost your mittens. Then act like you have found your mittens.

- Cats and kittens **meow** and **purr**.

Dogs and puppies _____and

_____.

Horses and colts _____ and

_____.

Pigs and piglets _____and

_____.

What sounds do other animals make?

_____

_____

_____

_____

_____

_____

- The three little kittens lost their mittens. Have you ever lost something? Draw a picture of the thing you lost. Draw a picture of where you found it.

# The North Wind

The north wind does blow,
And we will have snow,
What will poor Robin do then?
Poor thing!
He'll sit in a barn,
And keep himself warm,
And hide his head under his wing,
Poor thing!

**Directions:** Circle or write the answer to the following questions about the nursery rhyme.

1. The north wind is going to bring the—

   snow     rain     sun

2. Robin is a—

   boy     horse     bird     wind

3. What problem is Robin going to have?

   _____

   _____

   _____

4. Robin will hide his head because he—

   wants to stay warm

   is afraid

   wants to hide

5. Robin is a "poor thing" because he doesn't have any money.

   Yes     No

- Robin put his head under his wing. He did this to stay warm. How do these animals stay warm?

dog _____

cat _____

horse _____

cow _____

YOU! _____

- Draw a picture of the north wind.

- What kind of things can you find in a barn? Draw them in the barn.

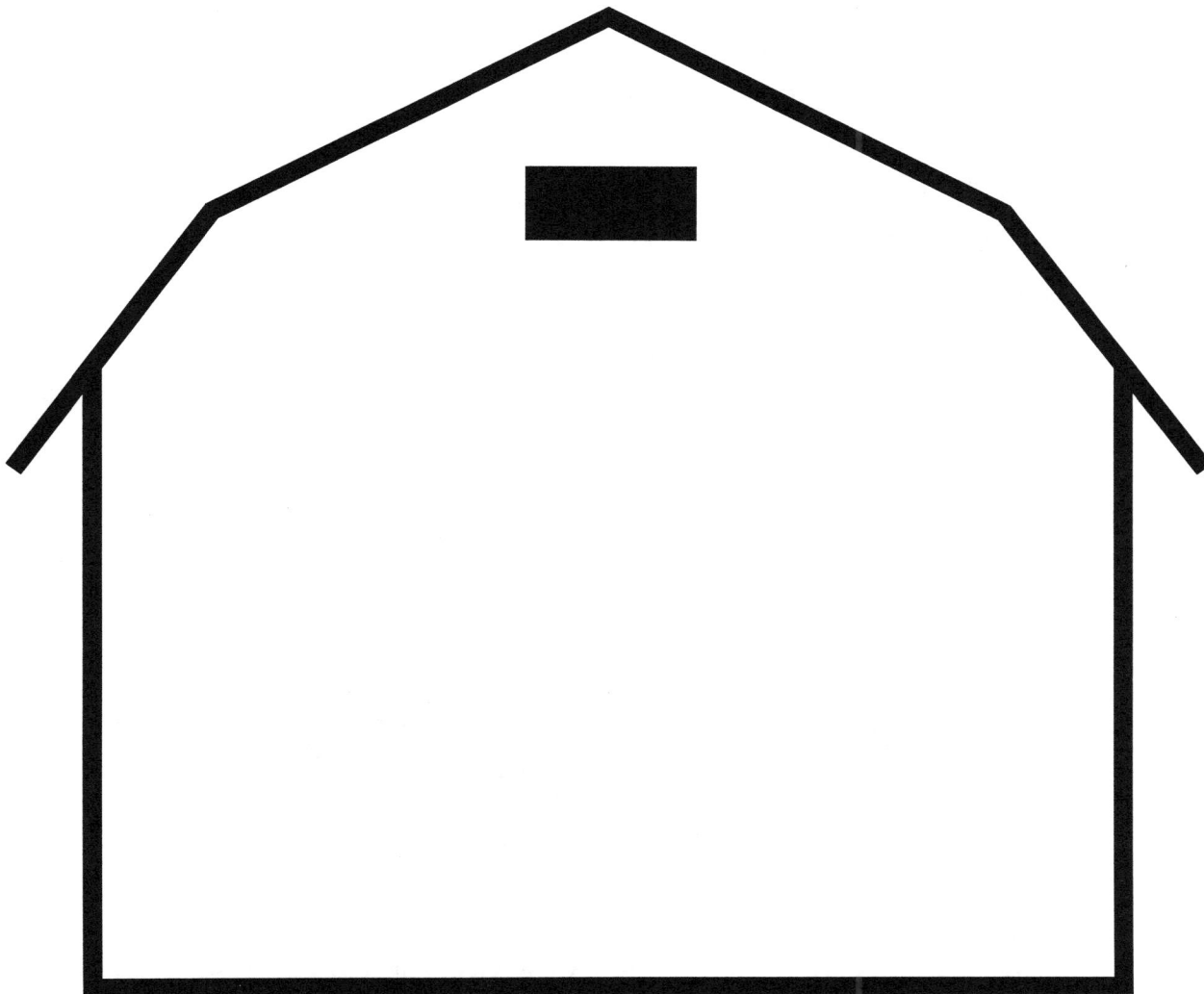

# Little Boy Blue

Little Boy Blue,
Come blow your horn,
The sheep's in the meadow,
The cow's in the corn.
Where is the boy
Who looks after the sheep?
He's under the haystack,
Fast asleep.

**Directions:** Circle or write the answer to the following questions about the nursery rhyme.

1. Where is Little Boy Blue?

   in the meadow     under the haystack     in the corn

2. What is Little Boy Blue doing?

   sleeping     talking     looking

3. What is Little Boy Blue's job?

   staying in the meadow

   watching the corn

   taking care of the sheep

4. Little Boy Blue should blow his horn because the cow is eating the corn.

   Yes     No

5. This poem is about something that probably happened in a city.

   Yes     No

- Write a new rhyme by putting new words in the blanks.

Little Boy Blue

Come _____ your _____ ,

The _____ in the _____ ,

The _____ in the _____ .

Where is the boy

Who looks after the _____ ?

He's under the _____

_____ .

- Little Boy Blue wouldn't wake up. List 3 ways you could make Little Boy Blue wake up.

_____

_____

_____

_____

_____

_____

_____

- Little Boy Blue played a horn by blowing on it. List other instruments in the right place on the chart.

## Musical Instruments

| Blow | Hit | Strum |
|------|-----|-------|
|      |     |       |
|      |     |       |
|      |     |       |
|      |     |       |
|      |     |       |
|      |     |       |
|      |     |       |
|      |     |       |
|      |     |       |
|      |     |       |
|      |     |       |
|      |     |       |

# Boys and Girls
# Come Out to Play

Boys and girls, come out to play,
The moon is shining as bright as day,
Leave your supper and leave your sleep,
And join your playmates in the street.
Come with a whoop and come with a call,
Come with a good will or don't come at all.
Up the ladder and down the wall,
A half-penny loaf will serve us all,
You find milk, and I'll find flour,
And we'll have pudding in half an hour.

**Directions:** Circle or write the answer to the following questions about the nursery rhyme.

1.  The boys and girls are going out at night.

    Yes      No

2.  The boys and girls will go up the—

    wall      ladder      street

3.  Who will join the boys and girls in the street?

    _____

4.  What kind of food are the boys and girls going to make?

    pudding      milk      flour

5.  The boys and girls will leave their _____

    and their _____ .

6.  The boys and girls will have enough light to play because—

    the stars are out

    the moon is shining

    they have a ladder

- What kind of games do you play outside? What kind of games do you play inside? What kind of games can you play outside or inside? List the games in the right part of the circles.

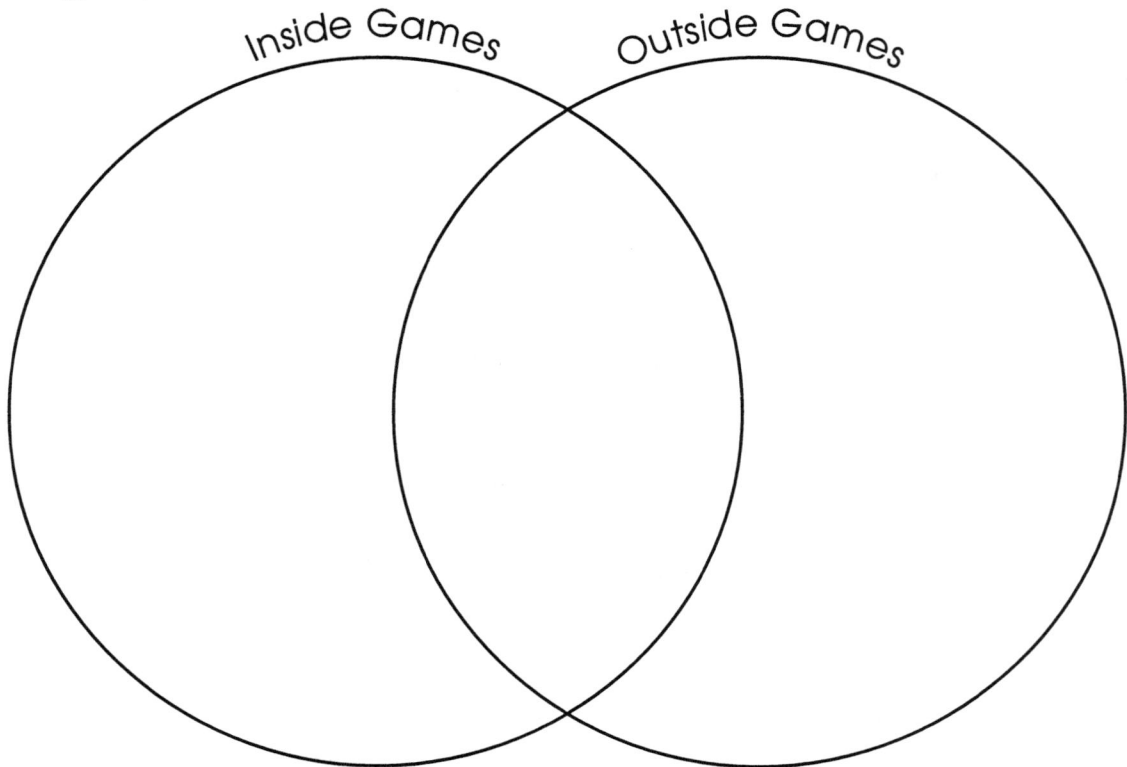

Inside Games          Outside Games

- The poem says that "the moon is shining as bright as day." Draw and color a picture of that moon.

- Act out this poem for your parents.

# Mary Had a Little Lamb

Mary had a little lamb,
Its **fleece** was white as snow.
And everywhere that Mary went
The lamb was sure to go.

It followed her to school one day,
Which was against the rules.
It made the children laugh and play
To see a lamb in school.

And so the teacher turned it out,
But still it did stay near
And waited quietly about
Until Mary did appear.

"What makes the lamb love Mary so?"
The other children cry.
"Because Mary loves the lamb, you know,"
The teacher did **reply**.

**Directions:** Circle or write the answer to the following questions about the nursery rhyme.

1. The word **fleece** means—

   snow      feet      girl      fur

2. The children laughed and played because Mary was funny.

   Yes      No

3. What did the teacher do with Mary's lamb?

   _____

   _____

4. Why did the lamb love Mary?

   _____

   _____

5. The word **reply** means—

   yell      answer      lamb

- The teacher did not want a lamb at school. What kind of problems would a lamb cause at school?

_____

_____

_____

_____

_____

- Finish these sentences.

A giraffe would make a great pet because _____

_____ .

A camel would make a great pet because _____

_____ .

A penguin would make a great pet because _____

_____ .

A_____would make a great pet because

_____ .

- The lamb was Mary's pet. Mary loved the lamb. How do people show that they love their pets? Draw pictures to answer the question.

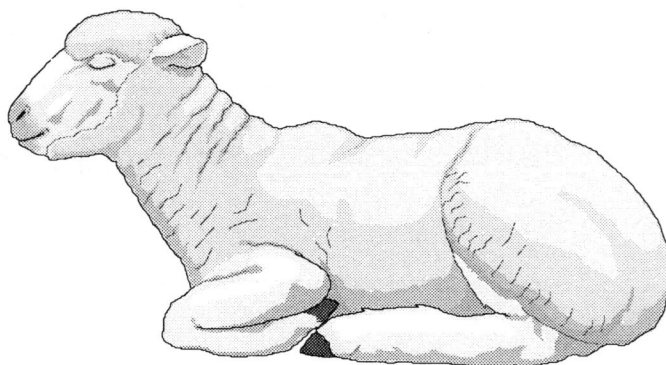

# Wee Willie Winkie

Wee Willie Winkie runs through the town,
Upstairs and downstairs in his nightgown,
**Rapping** on the window
Crying through the lock,
"Are the children all in bed
For now it's eight o'clock?"

**Directions:** Circle or write the answer to the following questions about the nursery rhyme.

1. Wee Willie Winkie ran through houses.

   Yes     No

2. What did Wee Willie Winkie wear?

   _____

3. The word **rapping** means—

   talking     tapping     walking

4. Why should the children be in bed?_____

   _____

   _____

- Draw a picture of Wee Willie Winkie.

- Wee Willie Winkie wanted children to be in bed at eight o'clock. Show eight o'clock on the first clock. Show your bedtime on the second clock.

- Pretend you are Wee Willie Winkie. Act out the poem for your family.

# Three Wishes and a Sausage

Once a poor man went for a walk in the woods. "Oh, dear," he said, "I'm so unhappy. My wife and I are living with no money."

Suddenly the man saw an elf. The elf said, "You poor man! I heard what you said. I want to help you. You may wish for whatever you like. Your first three wishes will be given to you."

The poor man was very happy. He ran home and **related** what happened to his wife. "How super!" she said.

"I can wish for a big house," said the man.

"I can wish for a maid to take care of our house," said the wife.

"I can wish for a horse," said the man.

"I can wish for pretty clothes," said the wife.

They were so excited, but they couldn't decide on their three wishes.

After a while, the man was hungry so he said, "I wish I had a sausage to eat." At once, a sausage fell on his plate.

"You foolish man," said the wife. "Why did you waste a wish on that?" She yelled and yelled about how foolish the man had been. Finally he got angry and said, "I wish this sausage were hanging from your nose!"

Just like that, the sausage was hanging from his wife's nose.

"Get it off!" she screamed. She tried to pull it off. The husband tried to yank it off. It would not move.

"I have one wish left," said the man.

"What good is a third wish when I have a sausage hanging from my nose?" asked the wife. "I look stupid. It is your fault."

"Don't cry," said her husband. "For my third wish I wish for the sausage to be off your nose."

Kerplop! The sausage dropped to the table. Then they sadly sat down and ate the sausage.

**Directions:** Circle or write the answer to the following questions about the story.

1. In this story, the word **related** means—

   hid       told       sang       ran

2. How did the wife feel when she had the sausage on her nose?

   happy       excited       angry       sad

3. What happened right after the man wished for a sausage?

   A sausage fell on his plate.

   The man saw an elf.

   The wife wished for a maid.

4. The wife wanted a horse to ride.

   Yes       No

5. This story is mostly about a man and woman who meet an elf.

   Yes       No

- You have three wishes. What will you wish for? Draw pictures of what you will wish for.

- What would you do if you had a sausage on your nose? Make up a dance that shows what you would do.

- Finish these sentences.

A wish is like a _____

_____.

A sausage is like a _____

_____.

An elf is like a _____

_____.

# A Lost Bird

Jim and his best friend George were playing hide-and-seek after supper.

"Come and look," Jim shouted. George ran to the tree where Jim stood. They saw a gray, fuzzy ball.

"It's a baby bird," George said.

"Where did it come from?" asked Jim.

"I think it fell from this tree," said George.

Jim's mother came into the yard. "What are you looking for?" she asked.

"Look, Mother. We found a baby bird," said Jim.

"It must have fallen from its nest during the storm last night," Jim's mother said. She walked over and carefully picked up the bird. She took it into the house. The boys were close behind her.

"Get a box and an old towel," she said. Jim found a box. He placed the towel in it. Then his mother placed the bird in the box.

"What can we feed the bird, Mother?" asked Jim.

"I'm not sure, Jim," she answered.

"I'll call Uncle Tim," said George. "He likes birds. He'll know what to feed a little bird." George called his uncle and talked to him. Then George came back.

"Uncle Tim said the baby bird can eat warm cereal and milk. We'll need an eye dropper. We will use it to feed the bird," George said. George and Jim watched the bird. Jim's mother made the warm cereal.

"Can I feed it?" asked Jim.

"Of course," answered his mother, "but take turns."

Jim and George put drops of food in the little bird's open mouth. When it did not eat anymore, they watched it fall asleep. Then they ran outside to play. They began their game again.

"It was fun to find a little bird, wasn't it, George?" asked Jim.

"Yes," said George, "and it feels good to help a little animal."

**Directions:** Circle or write the answer to the following questions about the story.

1. Uncle Tim told George to feed the bird with—

   an old towel        an eye dropper        a bottle

2. This story happened in the early morning.

   Yes        No

3. Which of these is a FACT?

   It's fun to find a little bird.

   Jim's mother made warm cereal for the baby bird.

4. The baby bird probably fell because a storm shook the tree.

   Yes        No

5. Jim and George will probably—

   give the baby bird to Uncle Tim

   take care of the bird until it is okay

# Supplement and Answer Key to
## *Reading and More*, Grade 1

### Hints for Using *Reading and More*

- Provide a special place where young readers can work and learn. Keep basic supplies and materials (a dictionary, paper, pencils, colors, etc.) within easy reach of young hands.

- Work and learn together. Many activities in this book invite family members to join in the learning. Young learners respond when they know others are interested in what they are doing.

- Nurture a positive attitude about reading. Make plenty of reading material available for all family members. Read with and to young learners. Read for your own enjoyment, too.

- Nurture a positive attitude about thinking. Extend the young learners' thinking by asking questions like the following: "Why do you think that is true?" "How did you come up with that answer?" "What else could you do with this information?" "Where have you seen something like this before?" Encourage young learners to ask themselves these kinds of questions, too.

- Challenge young learners to solve problems and find answers on their own. They can accomplish many things through persistence.

- Keep learning fun and challenging, but never frustrating. If something is too difficult, or if young learners become tired, put the activity away for another time.

- Try a positive incentive program. Reward young learners for completing lessons with stickers or some other appropriate treat. This book includes an "Achievement Award" for completing all the lessons. Celebrate successes, which come in many forms.

**Other books in the ECS Home Study Collection™—**

| Reading and More | Language Arts and More | Math and More |
|---|---|---|
| Grade 2 | Grade 1 | Grade 1 |
| Grade 3 | Grade 2 | Grade 2 |
| Grade 4 | Grade 3 | Grade 3 |
| Grade 5 | Grade 4 | Grade 4 |
| Grade 6 | Grade 5 | Grade 5 |
|  | Grade 6 | Grade 6 |

**Visit your local bookstore for these and other titles, or contact:**

ECS Learning Systems, Inc. • PO Box 791437 • San Antonio, TX 78279 • 1-800-688-3224

**Directions:** Circle or write the answer to the following questions about the nursery rhyme.

1. The three little kittens got in trouble because they—

   were fighting

   (lost their mittens)

   ate the pie

2. The word **naughty** means—

   good    happy    (bad)

3. The three little kittens could not have pie because—

   (they lost their mittens)

   they found their mittens

   they were crying

4. The mother cat gave the kittens pie after they found their mittens.

   (Yes)    No

5. What sound did the kittens make when they were happy?

   purr, purr

3

---

**Directions:** Circle or write the answer to the following questions about the nursery rhyme.

1. The north wind is going to bring the—

   (snow)    rain    sun

2. Robin is a—

   boy    horse    (bird)    wind

3. What problem is Robin going to have?

   He must keep warm.

   _____

4. Robin will hide his head because he—

   (wants to stay warm)

   is afraid

   wants to hide

5. Robin is a "poor thing" because he doesn't have any money.

   Yes    (No)

7

---

**Directions:** Circle or write the answer to the following questions about the nursery rhyme.

1. Where is Little Boy Blue?

   in the meadow    (under the haystack)    in the corn

2. What is Little Boy Blue doing?

   (sleeping)    talking    looking

3. What is Little Boy Blue's job?

   staying in the meadow

   watching the corn

   (taking care of the sheep)

4. Little Boy Blue should blow his horn because the cow is eating the corn.

   (Yes)    No

5. This poem is about something that probably happened in a city.

   Yes    (No)

11

---

**Directions:** Circle or write the answer to the following questions about the nursery rhyme.

1. The boys and girls are going out at night.

   (Yes)    No

2. The boys and girls will go up the—

   wall    (ladder)    street

3. Who will join the boys and girls in the street?

   their playmates

4. What kind of food are the boys and girls going to make?

   (pudding)    milk    flour

5. The boys and girls will leave their **supper** and their **sleep**

6. The boys and girls will have enough light to play because—

   the stars are out

   (the moon is shining)

   they have a ladder

15

---

**Directions:** Circle or write the answer to the following questions about the nursery rhyme.

1. The word **fleece** means—

   snow    feet    girl    (fur)

2. The children laughed and played because Mary was funny.

   Yes    (No)

3. What did the teacher do with Mary's lamb?

   She put it outside.

4. Why did the lamb love Mary?

   Mary loves the lamb.

   _____

5. The word **reply** means—

   yell    (answer)    lamb

18

---

**Directions:** Circle or write the answer to the following questions about the nursery rhyme.

1. Wee Willie Winkie ran through houses.

   Yes    (No)

2. What did Wee Willie Winkie wear?

   his nightgown

3. The word **rapping** means—

   talking    (tapping)    walking

4. Why should the children be in bed?

   It is eight o'clock.

   _____

22

---

**Directions:** Circle or write the answer to the following questions about the story.

1. In this story, the word **related** means—

   hid    (told)    sang    ran

2. How did the wife feel when she had the sausage on her nose?

   happy    excited    (angry)    sad

3. What happened right after the man wished for a sausage?

   (A sausage fell on his plate)

   The man saw an elf.

   The woman wished for a maid.

4. The wife wanted a horse to ride.

   Yes    (No)

5. This story is mostly about a man and woman who meet an elf.

   Yes    (No)

26

---

**Directions:** Circle or write the answer to the following questions about the story.

1. Uncle Tim told George to feed the bird with—

   an old towel    (an eye dropper)    a bottle

2. This story happened in the early morning.

   Yes    (No)

3. Which of these is a FACT?

   It's fun to find a little bird.

   (Jim's mother made warm cereal for the baby bird.)

4. The baby bird probably fell because a storm shook the tree.

   (Yes)    No

5. Jim and George will probably—

   give the baby bird to Uncle Tim

   (take care of the bird until it is okay)

30

---

**Directions:** Circle or write the answer to the following questions about the passage.

1. The word **blend** means—

   beat quickly

   (mix together)

   remove from the bowl

2. What do you do after you push the flour mixture to the sides of the bowl?

   pour in the oil

   pour in the milk

   (pour in the egg mixture)

3. When you make these muffins, you should bake them at 25 degrees.

   Yes    (No)

4. Another good title for this passage would be—

   (Making Blueberry Muffins)

   Rules for Cooking

   An Easy Recipe

33

**Directions:** Circle or write the answer to the following questions about the story.

1. The word **cruel** means—

   angry    sad    (mean)    funny

2. Who did the father and son see right after they started walking?

   **some old men** _____

3. Most of this story happened on a farm.

   Yes    (No)

4. The father and son carried the mule because the young woman told them to carry it.

   (Yes)    No

5. At the end of the story, the father will probably carry the mule again.

   Yes    (No)

37

---

**Directions:** Circle or write the answer to the following questions about the passage.

1. How do you use **bindings**? **They let you fasten boots to skis.** _____

2. What is the hardest thing about learning to ski?

   learning how to start    (learning how to stop)

3. Why do people go to ski classes?

   **to learn how to ski** _____

4. Most of this passage was about why people fall down.

   Yes    (No)

5. What are beginners?

   skiers on a hill

   (people just starting to learn skills)

   people who teach others

41

---

**Directions:** Circle or write the answer to the following questions about the passage.

1. The panda bear comes from **China** _____.

2. Panda bears live in bamboo forests because—

   people put them there

   (bamboo is their favorite food)

   they are small animals

3. A baby panda bear is called a _____ **cub** _____.

4. A panda bear never leaves its mother.

   Yes    (No)

5. When a panda bear grows up, how tall will it be?

   6 inches    (5 feet)    200 feet

44

---

**Directions:** Circle or write the answer to the following questions about the passage.

1. A panda bear's favorite food is—

   rice    carrots    apples    (bamboo)

2. Panda bears only eat bamboo.

   Yes    (No)

3. Why does a panda bear pull bark from the trees?

   (to mark its home)

   to make a bed

   to find food

4. Panda bears live in large groups.

   Yes    (No)

5. There is less bamboo for panda bears to eat because people are chopping down the bamboo forests.

   (Yes)    No

46

---

**Directions:** Circle or write the answer to the following questions about the passage.

1. The word **wise** means—

   old    round    (smart)    big

2. Owls are very **wise**.

   Yes    (No)

3. Most owls have bright colors.

   Yes    (No)

4. The snowy owl looks like snow because it—

   (has white feathers)

   has many feathers

   is very soft

5. Sometimes it looks like owls don't have a necks because—

   owls look at you a long time

   (owls have a thick layer of feathers)

   most owls are brown

50

---

**Directions:** Circle or write the answer to the following questions about the passage.

1. The word **talons** means—

   eyes    ears    (claws)    owls

2. All owls are the same size.

   Yes    (No)

3. How does good hearing help owls hunt?

   It lets them sleep at night.

   It lets them see small animals.

   (It lets them hear soft sounds.)

4. An owl eats small animals like **mice** _____ and **frogs** _____.

5. Where does the elf owl live? _____

   **North America** _____

52

---

**Directions:** Circle or write the answer to the following questions about the passage.

1. A **seedling** is a—

   small seed    (small plant)    small insect

2. The small cactus plant grows best in the hot sun.

   Yes    (No)

3. Where does the saguaro cactus grow?

   **Sonoran Desert** _____

4. A saguaro cactus can be _____ **50** _____ feet tall.

5. A saguaro cactus does not need water.

   Yes    (No)

6. The cactus seed grows best in _____ **rocky** _____ dirt.

55

---

**Directions:** Circle or write the answer to the following questions about the passage.

1. The saguaro cactus grows its arms when it is _____ **35** _____ years old.

2. A saguaro cactus does not grow after it is 6 years old.

   Yes    (No)

3. The saguaro cactus blooms at night because—

   the white flowers make red fruit

   (the sun is too hot for the flowers)

   the cactus lives for many years

4. The fruit on the cactus is—

   white    purple    (red)

5. The saguaro cactus is a "giant" because it—

   (is 50 feet tall)

   is 150 years old

   has white flowers

57

This checklist highlights the reading skills needed to answer objective questions for each passage.

**vocabulary:** determining the meanings of words in context
**facts & details:** recalling important information from the passage
**sequencing:** recalling the sequential order of events in the passage
**following directions:** understanding written directions in the passage
**main idea:** identifying the stated or implied main idea of the passage
**cause/effect:** understanding cause and effect relationships
**predicting:** predicting probable future events from information in the passage
**generalizing:** understanding general ideas and making inferences from information in the passage
**fact/opinion:** understanding the difference between fact and opinion

| | Vocabulary | Facts & Details | Sequencing | Following Directions | Main Idea | Cause/Effect | Predicting | Generalizing | Fact/Opinion |
|---|---|---|---|---|---|---|---|---|---|
| Three Little Kittens p. 2 | ✓ | ✓ | ✓ | | ✓ | | ✓ | | |
| The North Wind p. 6 | | ✓ | | | ✓ | | ✓ | | |
| Little Boy Blue p. 10 | | ✓ | | | ✓ | | ✓ | | |
| Boys and Girls Come Out... p. 14 | | ✓ | | | ✓ | | ✓ | | |
| Mary Had a Little Lamb p.17 | ✓ | ✓ | | | ✓ | | | | |
| Wee Willie Winkie p. 21 | ✓ | ✓ | | | ✓ | | | | |
| Three Wishes and a Sausage p. 24 | ✓ | ✓ | ✓ | ✓ | | | ✓ | | |
| A Lost Bird p. 28 | | ✓ | | | ✓ | ✓ | | ✓ | |
| How to Make Blueberry ... p. 32 | ✓ | | ✓ | ✓ | ✓ | | | | |
| A Father, a Son, and a Mule p. 35 | ✓ | ✓ | ✓ | | ✓ | ✓ | | | |
| Snow Skiing is Fun! p. 39 | ✓ | ✓ | | ✓ | ✓ | | ✓ | | |
| What Is a Panda Bear? p. 43 | ✓ | ✓ | | | ✓ | | | | |
| More About Panda Bears p. 45 | | ✓ | | | ✓ | | ✓ | | |
| Some Facts About Owls p. 49 | ✓ | ✓ | | | ✓ | | | ✓ | |
| More Facts About Owls p. 51 | ✓ | ✓ | | | | | ✓ | | |
| A Giant Cactus p. 54 | ✓ | ✓ | | | | | ✓ | | |
| More About the Saguaro p. 56 | | ✓ | ✓ | | ✓ | | ✓ | | |

✂ - - - - - - - - - - - - - - - - - - - - - - - - - - - - - - - - - - - - -

### The Home Study Team would like to recognize your child's achievement!

After your child successfully finishes this book, ask him/her to write a brief letter that explains what (s)he liked about the book and learned from completing the activities. Mail the child's letter and this completed coupon to: Home Study Team, ECS, PO Box 791437, San Antonio, TX 78279. **Include a legal-size, stamped, self-addressed envelope.** The Home Study Team will send:

- for the child—an embossed seal to attach to his/her Achievement Award
- for the parent—an informative pamphlet with more ideas for helping your child learn

Parent's Name _____

Address _____

City_____ State _____ Zip _____

Child's Name _____ Child's Age _____

Book Completed (circle one):     Reading          Language Arts          Math

Grade Level (circle one):     1          2          3          4          5          6

- What would be a good name for the baby bird? List as many names as you can.

  _____

  _____

  _____

- Pet birds live in cages. Draw the "perfect" cage for a pet bird.

- Go outside and listen to the birds where you live. How do they sound? Try to make sounds like the birds you hear.

# How to Make Blueberry Muffins

Ingredients:

one egg
one-half cup milk
one-fourth cup cooking oil
one and one-half cups flour
one-third cup sugar

two teaspoons
  baking powder
one-half teaspoon salt
one cup fresh or frozen
  blueberries

1.  In a small bowl, beat together the egg, milk, and cooking oil. Set mixture aside.

2.  In a large bowl, mix together flour, sugar, baking powder, and salt.

3.  Push the flour mixture to the sides of the bowl.

4.  Pour the egg mixture in the middle of the flour. Stir enough just to moisten the dry ingredients.

5.  Gently **blend** in the blueberries.

6.  Spoon the batter into greased muffin cups. Fill each one about two-thirds full.

7.  Bake the muffins in a 400-degree oven for 20 to 25 minutes, or until they are golden brown.

8.  When finished, take the muffins from the oven. Serve them hot with butter.

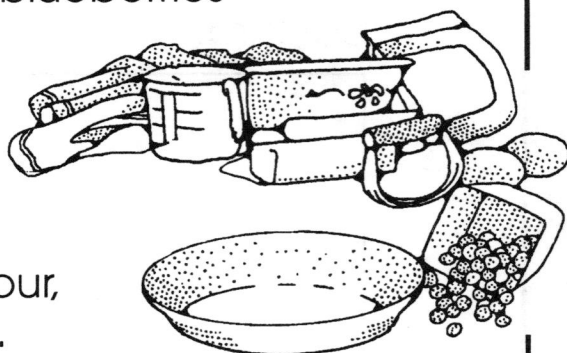

**Directions:** Circle or write the answer to the following questions about the passage.

1. The word **blend** means—

   beat quickly

   mix together

   remove from the bowl

2. What do you do after you push the flour mixture to the sides of the bowl?

   pour in the oil

   pour in the milk

   pour in the egg mixture

3. When you make these muffins, you should bake them at 25 degrees.

   Yes     No

4. Another good title for this passage would be—

   Making Blueberry Muffins

   Rules for Cooking

   An Easy Recipe

- Make blueberry muffins. Ask your mom or dad to help you.

- List things that are the same color as blueberries.

_____

_____

List things that are as small as blueberries.

_____

_____

- You need eggs to make blueberry muffins. Eggs come from chickens. Ask your mom or dad to help you finish these sentences.

Milk comes from _____ .

Sugar comes from _____ .

Flour comes from _____ .

Cooking oil comes from _____ .

Blueberries come from _____ .

Salt comes from _____ .

# A Father, a Son, and a Mule

A long time ago, a father and son were walking to town with their mule. They had not gone far when they met some old men. The men began laughing at the father and son.

"Why are you laughing?" asked the father.

"Foolish man," said one old man. "You walk when you could ride."

The father got on the mule and began to ride. His son walked beside him. Soon the father and son met some old women. They began throwing rocks at the father.

"Why are you throwing rocks at me?" asked the father.

"You **cruel** man!" yelled one old woman. "You make your son walk."

The father got off and put his son on the mule. His son rode and he walked beside him. Soon they met a group of children. The children pointed at the father and son.

"Why are you pointing?" asked the father.

"Silly people!" said one child. "One walks when you both could ride."

The father jumped on the mule and rode away with his son. Before too long, they met a young woman. She began beating them with a broom.

"Why are you beating us?" asked the father.

"You **cruel** people!" yelled the young woman. "You both ride this poor mule. You should carry the animal."

The father and son jumped off the mule. They picked up the mule and began carrying it down the road. Soon they met an old farmer. The farmer just shook his head.

"Why are you shaking your head?" asked the father.

"Such stupid people! Why would you carry a mule? The father should ride him," said the farmer.

The father and son looked at each other. They set the mule on his feet and finished their walk to town without asking any more questions.

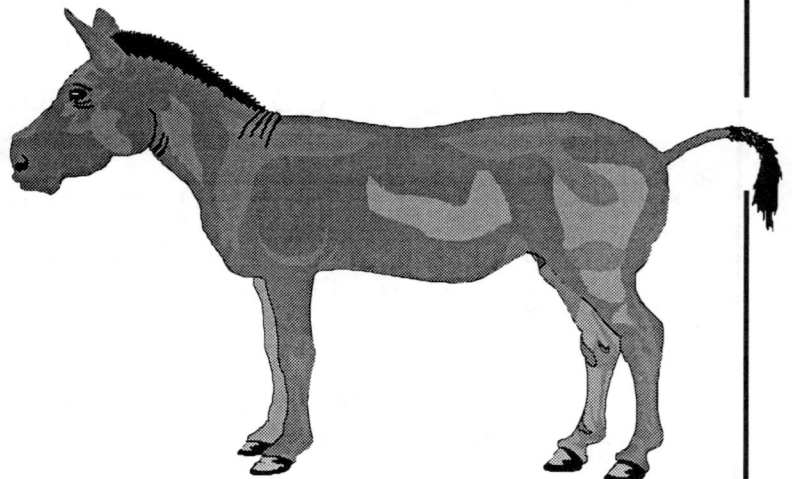

**Directions:** Circle or write the answer to the following questions about the story.

1. The word **cruel** means—

    angry        sad        mean        funny

2. Who did the father and son see right after they started walking?

    _____

3. Most of this story happened on a farm.

    Yes        No

4. The father and son carried the mule because the young woman told them to carry it.

    Yes        No

5. At the end of the story, the father will probably carry the mule again.

    Yes        No

- Pretend that the man's mule could talk. What would he say to the man and the boy?

_____

_____

- Pretend that the man and his son had an elephant. How would the story be different? Draw a picture that shows how the story would be different.

- Use the tune to "Old MacDonald Had a Farm." Make up new words about the father, his son, and their mule.

_____

_____

Hello!

_____

_____

# Snow Skiing Is Fun!

Have you ever been snow skiing? It can be scary. It can also be fun!

First, you need lots of snow. Many places in the United States do not have enough snow. You may have to travel to another state. Colorado and New Mexico have great ski areas. The roads to the ski slopes are kept clear of snow. This makes it safe to drive. It is also beautiful to drive through the snowy mountains.

You can sign up for classes at the ski resort. You can also rent skis, boots, and **bindings**. **Bindings** let you fasten your boots to the skis. Ski boots are hard to walk in, but they keep your feet warm. They help protect your ankles when you fall, too.

You must learn how to move with skis on your feet. It is

important to know how to start, turn, and stop. When you start down a hill, you move fast. Stopping is the hardest thing to learn when you ski. If you don't know how to stop, you fall. Most people go to classes and learn these skills. All the **beginners** in class fall down. Everyone laughs a lot.

Falling in soft snow doesn't hurt. But, it is not easy to get up with skis on your feet. It is hard to move up the hill, too. After you learn to start, turn, and stop, you can ride a ski lift to the top of a hill. Then you can ski down. Most people fall many times on the way down. Falling is the surest way to stop!

Even if you don't ski down the slope, it's fun to learn to ski. It's fun to fall and play in the snow.

**Directions:** Circle or write the answer to the following questions about the passage.

1. How do you use **bindings**? _____

_____

2. What is the hardest thing about learning to ski?

learning how to start      learning how to stop

3. Why do people go to ski classes? _____

_____

4. Most of this passage was about why people fall down.

Yes      No

5. What are **beginners**?

skiers on a hill

people just starting to learn skills

people who teach others

- How do you think it feels to ski? Pretend you are skiing. Act out skiing down a hill.

- Snow is cold, white, and soft. Finish the sentences. Try to think of answers no one else would write.

  Snow is as cold as _____ .

  Snow is as white as _____ .

  Snow is as soft as _____ .

- Snow and rain are alike in some ways. Snow and rain are different in some ways. Think about how snow and rain are alike and different. Write your ideas in the right place on the chart.

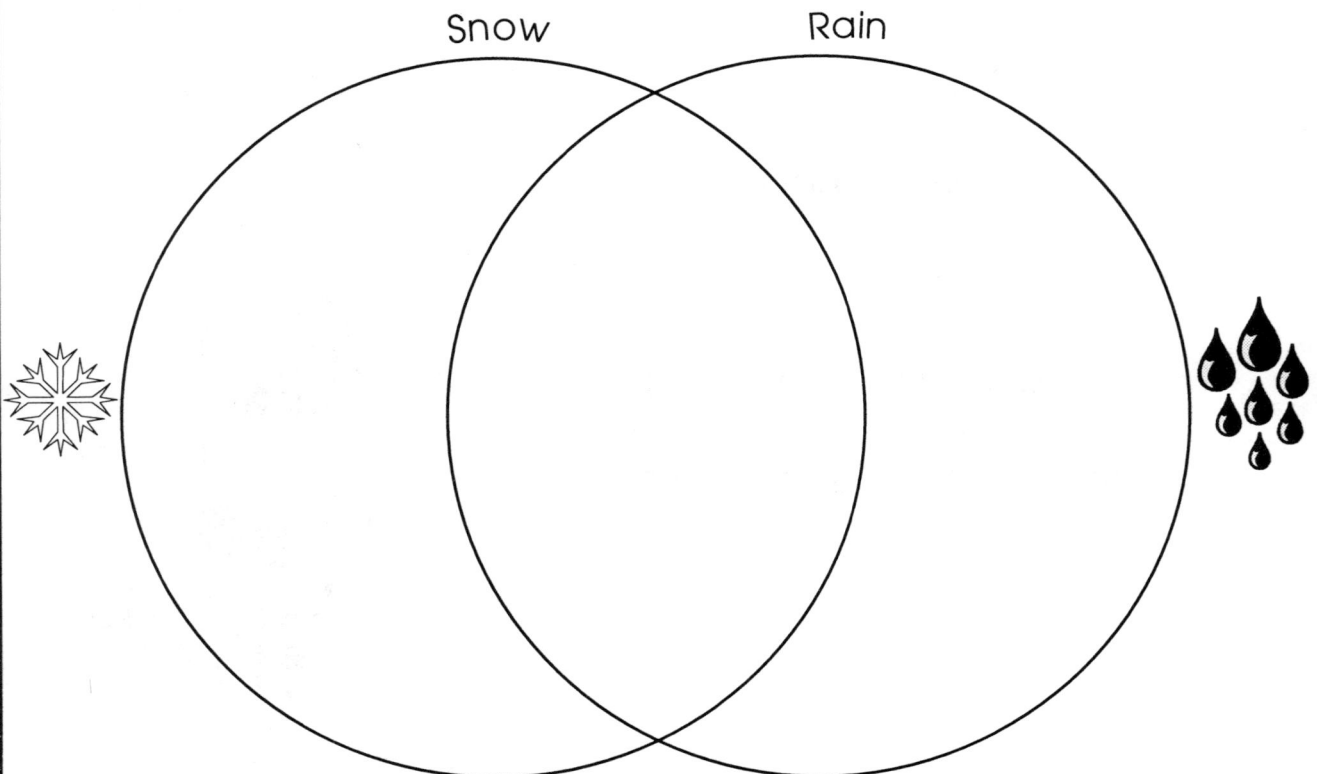

Snow                 Rain

# What Is a Panda Bear?

Do you like panda bears? Many people do.

The panda bear comes from China. It lives high in the hills and mountains. It lives in the bamboo forests. Bamboo is the panda's favorite kind of food.

What is a panda bear? Some people think it is like a raccoon. Other people think it is more like a bear. People in China call it a "bear-cat."

A baby panda bear is called a **cub**. A **cub** is very small. It is only 6 inches long. You could hold it in your hand. The little **cub** cannot see. It has very fine hair on its body. The **cub** lives with its mother for about 18 months. Then it can live without its mother. When it grows up, it will be about 5 feet tall. It will weigh about 200-250 pounds.

**Directions:** Circle or write the answer to the following questions about the passage.

1. The panda bear comes from _____.

2. Panda bears live in bamboo forests because—

   people put them there

   bamboo is their favorite food

   they are small animals

3. A baby panda bear is called a _____.

4. A panda bear never leaves its mother.

   Yes     No

5. When a panda bear grows up, how tall will it be?

   6 inches     5 feet     200 feet

# More About Panda Bears

Panda bears like bamboo. It is their favorite food. A panda bear can eat 50 pounds of bamboo in one day! Some panda bears live in zoos. They eat other kinds of food. They can eat carrots, apples, and rice.

Panda bears like to live alone. They try to keep other panda bears away. They put their scent, or smell, on trees. They pull bark from the trees. This is how they mark their home. Other pandas leave them alone.

Today there are only about 1000 panda bears on earth. Where did the panda bears go? Why are there only 1000 panda bears? There are many reasons. People have cut down the bamboo forests. There is less bamboo for the panda bears to eat. Some people hunt and trap panda bears. Many baby panda bears die when they are young.

**Directions:** Circle or write the answer to the following questions about the passage.

1.  A panda bear's favorite food is—

    rice        carrots        apples        bamboo

2.  Panda bears only eat bamboo.

    Yes        No

3.  Why does a panda bear pull bark from the trees?

    to mark its home

    to make a bed

    to find food

4.  Panda bears live in large groups.

    Yes        No

5.  There is less bamboo for panda bears to eat because people are chopping down the bamboo forests.

    Yes        No

- Panda bears like to be alone. List 3 funny reasons why panda bears like to be alone.

_____

_____

_____

_____

_____

_____

- Look at the map. Where is China? Ask your mom or dad to help you find China. Color it green. Color your country blue.

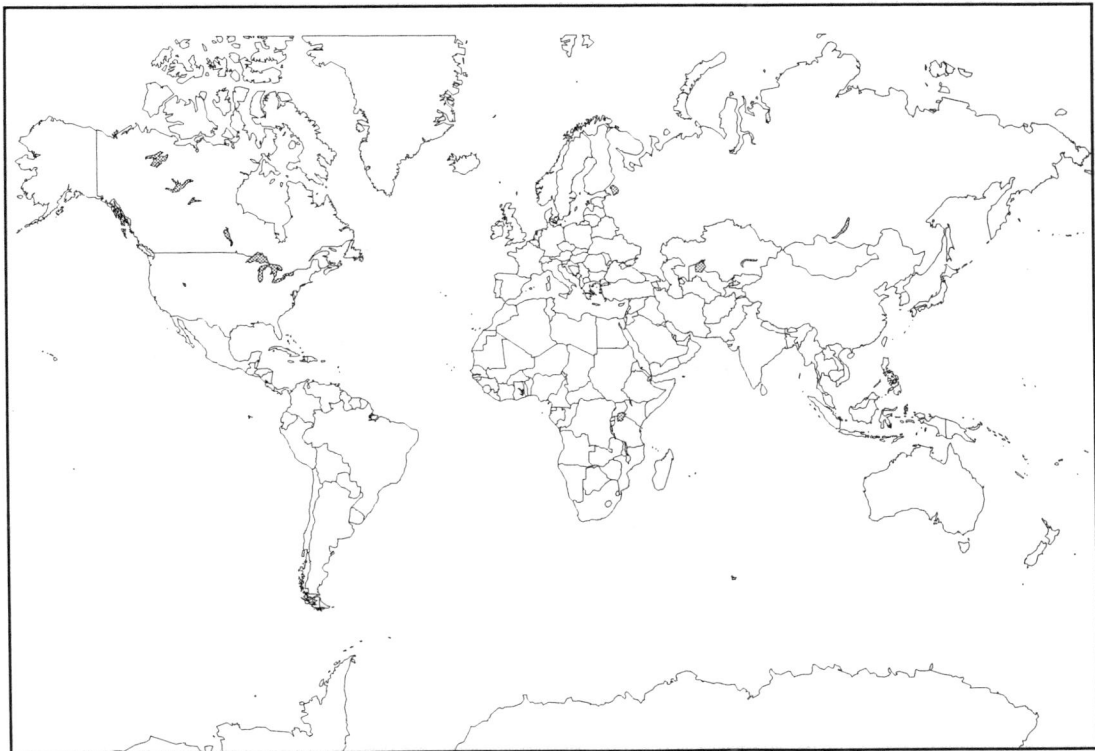

- Panda bears eat bamboo. It is their favorite food. People make things from bamboo. Can you find something in your house that is made from bamboo? List things that can be made from bamboo.

_____

_____

_____

_____

_____

# Some Facts About Owls

Have you ever seen an owl? An owl has a very special look. It has a large, round head. Its eyes are very big and set in the front of its head. So it seems like the owl is looking at you all the time. Some people say that an owl looks **wise**, or smart.

Sometimes it looks like an owl doesn't have a neck. This is because the owl has a very thick layer of feathers. Some owls have a ring of feathers around each eye. The rings look like eyeglasses.

Most owls are not very colorful. They have gray, tan, or brown feathers. Some owls have other colors. The snowy owl lives in a place that is very cold and snowy. It has white feathers. It looks like the snow.

**Directions:** Circle or write the answer to the following questions about the passage.

1. The word **wise** means—

   old      round      smart      big

2. Owls are very **wise**.

   Yes      No

3. Most owls have bright colors.

   Yes      No

4. The snowy owl looks like snow because it—

   has white feathers

   has many feathers

   is very soft

5. Sometimes it looks like owls don't have necks because—

   owls look at you a long time

   owls have a thick layer of feathers

   most owls are brown

# More Facts About Owls

Owls come in many sizes. The eagle owl lives in Africa and Asia. It is very big. It can be 30 inches high. It weighs more than 5 pounds. The elf owl is very small. It is only about 5 inches long. It lives in North America.

Most owls hunt at night. They hunt for small animals like mice and frogs. They catch the animals with their sharp claws. Their claws are called **talons**. Owls can see very well in the dark. Their big eyes let them see many things. This makes it easy to see the small animals.

Owls can hear very well. Feathers cover their ears. They use the feathers to help them hear from different places. An owl can hear a soft sound from far away. This helps owls hunt, too.

Owls are interesting birds. Maybe someday you will see one near your home!

**Directions:** Circle or write the answer to the following questions about the passage.

1.  The word **talons** means—

    eyes     ears     claws     owls

2.  All owls are the same size.

    Yes     No

3.  How does good hearing help owls hunt?

    It lets them sleep at night.

    It lets them see small animals.

    It lets them hear soft sounds.

4.  An owl eats small animals like _____

    and _____ .

5.  Where does the elf owl live? _____

    _____

- Some people say that an owl looks wise, or smart. Stand in front of a mirror. Pretend you are an owl. Make "owl faces." Do you look smart?

- Color this picture of an owl. Remember that most owls are not very colorful.

- Write a story about an owl that lives in your back yard.

_____

_____

_____

_____

_____

# A Giant Cactus

Some cactus plants are small. Some cactus plants are big. One of the biggest cactus plants is the saguaro cactus. This cactus plant grows in the Sonoran Desert. It can be 50 feet tall. It can weigh 20,000 pounds.

A saguaro cactus starts as a small, black seed. The seed grows best in rocky dirt. This kind of dirt holds water for the seed. It also keeps the wind away from the seed. Some animals and insects like to eat the small, black seeds. The rocky dirt hides the seeds. Animals and insects cannot see them.

The small, black seed grows into a small cactus plant. The small plant is a **seedling**. Hot sun can hurt the **seedling**. Too much heat will kill it. The small plant needs shade from the sun. It grows best in the shadow of a bigger cactus plant.

**Directions:** Circle or write the answer to the following questions about the passage.

1. A **seedling** is a—

   small seed        small plant        small insect

2. The small cactus plant grows best in the hot sun.

   Yes        No

3. Where does the saguaro cactus grow?

   _____

4. A saguaro cactus can be _____ feet tall.

5. A saguaro cactus does not need water.

   Yes        No

6. The cactus seed grows best in _____ dirt.

# More About the Saguaro

The saguaro cactus does not grow fast. In two years it will be only one inch tall. In ten years it may be six inches tall. It may have its first "arms" when it is 35 years old. A saguaro cactus can live for many years. Some are more than 150 years old. These are the "giants" that stand 50 feet tall.

In the spring, the saguaro cactus has white flowers. The desert sun is too hot for the flowers. They bloom at night. The white flowers make a red fruit. Many animals in the desert like to eat this fruit. Some people use the fruit to make syrup and wine.

**Directions:** Circle or write the answer to the following questions about the passage.

1. The saguaro cactus grows its arms when it is _____ years old.

2. A saguaro cactus does not grow after it is 6 years old.

   Yes     No

3. The saguaro cactus blooms at night because—

   the white flowers make red fruit

   the sun is too hot for the flowers

   the cactus lives for many years

4. The fruit on the cactus is—

   white     purple     red

5. The saguaro cactus is a "giant" because it—

   is 50 feet tall

   is 150 years old

   has white flowers

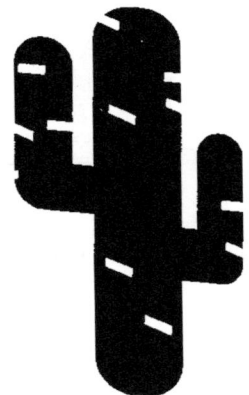

- The small cactus plant needs shade. Go outside and stand in the sun. Then stand in the shade. How did it feel in the sun? How did it feel in the shade?

| In the Shade | In the Sun |
|---|---|
|  |  |

- Look at a picture of a saguaro cactus. What does it look like? Finish these sentences.

A saguaro cactus looks like _____

_____ .

A saguaro cactus looks like _____

_____ .

A saguaro cactus looks like _____

_____ .

- Cactus plants grow in the desert. What else grows in a desert? What kind of animals live in a desert? Draw a desert picture. Show the plants and animals that are in a desert.

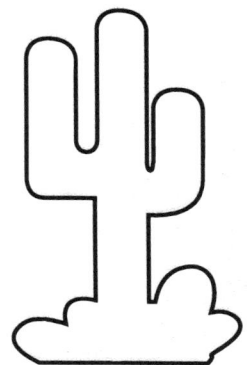

# Achievement Award

This award is presented to

_____

for successfully completing

**Reading and More**, Grade 1

Presented this _____ day of _____, 19 ____

_____

by

signature